VIOLIN

Intermediate Scales AND Bowings

for STRINGS

by HARVEY S. WHISTLER and HERMAN A. HUMMEL

CONTENTS

RUBANK®

HAL•LEONARD® CORPORATION
7777 W. BLUEMOUND RD. P.O. BOX 13819 MILWAUKEE, WI 53213

Key of C Major

Détaché Scale

Use détaché bowing in (1) LOWER HALF, (2) MIDDLE, and (3) UPPER HALF of bow.

Relative Minor Scales and Chords

Use détaché bowing in (1) LOWER HALF, (2) MIDDLE, and (3) UPPER HALF of bow.

Scales and Chords in Eighth Notes

Also practice (1) slurring each two notes, and (2) slurring each four notes.

Staccato Scales

Use short strokes in (1) LOWER HALF, and (2) MIDDLE of bow.

Scale and Chord in 6/8 Meter

Triplets

Use (1) LOWER HALF, (2) MIDDLE, and (3) UPPER HALF of bow.

Dotted Eighth and Sixteenth Notes

Use (1) LOWER HALF, (2) MIDDLE, and (3) UPPER HALF of bow. Also practice at the FROG with a separate bow for each note.

Be sure to start UP BOW. Play at extreme tip of stick, using about four inches of hair.

Articulated Scales and Chords

3

Key of G Major

Détaché Scale

Relative Minor Scales and Chords

Scales and Chords in Eighth Notes

Staccato Scales

4

Scale and Chord in 6/8 Meter

Triplets

Use (1) LOWER HALF, (2) MIDDLE, and (3) UPPER HALF of bow.

Dotted Eighth and Sixteenth Notes

Use (1) LOWER HALF, (2) MIDDLE, and (3) UPPER HALF of bow. Also practice at the FROG with a separate bow for each note.

Be sure to start UP BOW. Play at extreme tip of stick, using about four inches of hair.

Articulated Scales and Chords

Key of D Major

Détaché Scale

Use détaché bowing in (1) *LOWER HALF*, (2) *MIDDLE*, and (3) *UPPER HALF* of bow.

Relative Minor Scales and Chords

Use détaché bowing in (1) *LOWER HALF*, (2) *MIDDLE*, and (3) *UPPER HALF* of bow.

Scales and Chords in Eighth Notes

Also practice (1) slurring each two notes, and (2) slurring each four notes.

Staccato Scales

Use short strokes in (1) *LOWER HALF*, and (2) *MIDDLE* of bow.

Scale and Chord in 6/8 Meter

Triplets

Use (1) LOWER HALF, (2) MIDDLE, and (3) UPPER HALF of bow.

Dotted Eighth and Sixteenth Notes

Use (1) LOWER HALF, (2) MIDDLE, and (3) UPPER HALF of bow. Also practice at the FROG with a separate bow for each note.

Be sure to start UP BOW. Play at extreme tip of stick, using about four inches of hair.

AT POINT

Articulated Scales and Chords

LH   M   LH   FR

Key of A Major

Détaché Scale

49

Scale of A

Chord of A

Use détaché bowing in (1) LOWER HALF, (2) MIDDLE, and (3) UPPER HALF of bow.

Relative Minor Scales and Chords

Use détaché bowing in (1) LOWER HALF, (2) MIDDLE, and (3) UPPER HALF of bow.

50

F# Harmonic Minor

F# Minor

51

F# Melodic Minor

F# Minor

Scales and Chords in Eighth Notes

Also practice (1) slurring each two notes, and (2) slurring each four notes.

52

A Major

A Major

53

F# Harmonic Minor

F# Minor

54

F# Melodic Minor

F# Minor

Staccato Scales

Use short strokes in (1) LOWER HALF, and (2) MIDDLE of bow.

55

simile

56

Scale and Chord in 6/8 Meter

Triplets

Use (1) LOWER HALF, (2) MIDDLE, and (3) UPPER HALF of bow.

Dotted Eighth and Sixteenth Notes

Use (1) LOWER HALF, (2) MIDDLE, and (3) UPPER HALF of bow. Also practice at the FROG with a separate bow for each note.

Be sure to start UP BOW. Play at extreme tip of stick, using about four inches of hair.

Articulated Scales and Chords

9

Key of F Major

Détaché Scale

Use détaché bowing in (1) LOWER HALF, (2) MIDDLE, and (3) UPPER HALF of bow.

Relative Minor Scales and Chords

Use détaché bowing in (1) LOWER HALF, (2) MIDDLE, and (3) UPPER HALF of bow.

Scales and Chords in Eighth Notes

Also practice (1) slurring each two notes, and (2) slurring each four notes.

Staccato Scales

Use short strokes in (1) LOWER HALF, and (2) MIDDLE of bow.

Scale and Chord in 6/8 Meter

Triplets

Use (1) LOWER HALF, (2) MIDDLE, and (3) UPPER HALF of bow.

Dotted Eighth and Sixteenth Notes

Use (1) LOWER HALF, (2) MIDDLE, and (3) UPPER HALF of bow. Also practice at the FROG with a separate bow for each note.

Be sure to start UP BOW. Play at extreme tip of stick, using about four inches of hair.

Articulated Scales and Chords

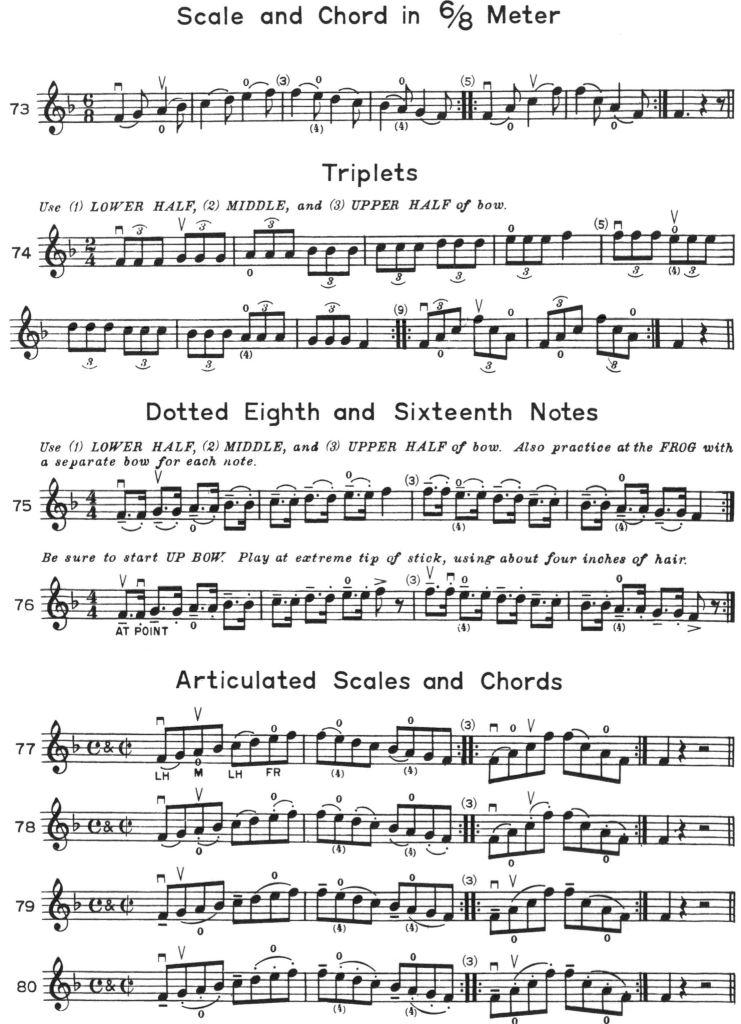

Key of B♭ Major

Détaché Scale

Use détaché bowing in (1) LOWER HALF, (2) MIDDLE, and (3) UPPER HALF of bow.

Relative Minor Scales and Chords

Use détaché bowing in (1) LOWER HALF, (2) MIDDLE, and (3) UPPER HALF of bow.

Scales and Chords in Eighth Notes

Also practice (1) slurring each two notes, and (2) slurring each four notes.

Staccato Scales

Use short strokes in (1) LOWER HALF, and (2) MIDDLE of bow.

12

Scale and Chord in 6/8 Meter

Triplets

Use (1) LOWER HALF, (2) MIDDLE, and (3) UPPER HALF of bow.

Dotted Eighth and Sixteenth Notes

Use (1) LOWER HALF, (2) MIDDLE, and (3) UPPER HALF of bow. Also practice at the FROG with a separate bow for each note.

Be sure to start UP BOW. Play at extreme tip of stick, using about four inches of hair.

AT POINT

Articulated Scales and Chords

LH M   LH   FR

Key of E♭ Major

Détaché Scale

Use détaché bowing in (1) LOWER HALF, (2) MIDDLE, and (3) UPPER HALF of bow.

Relative Minor Scales and Chords

Use détaché bowing in (1) LOWER HALF, (2) MIDDLE, and (3) UPPER HALF of bow.

Scales and Chords in Eighth Notes

Also practice (1) slurring each two notes, and (2) slurring each four notes.

Staccato Scales

Use short strokes in (1) LOWER HALF, and (2) MIDDLE of bow.

Scale and Chord in 6/8 Meter

Triplets

Use (1) LOWER HALF, (2) MIDDLE, and (3) UPPER HALF of bow.

Dotted Eighth and Sixteenth Notes

Use (1) LOWER HALF, (2) MIDDLE, and (3) UPPER HALF of bow. Also practice at the FROG with a separate bow for each note.

Be sure to start UP BOW. Play at extreme tip of stick, using about four inches of hair.

AT POINT

Articulated Scales and Chords

LH   M   LH   FR

Chromatic Scales

FIRST POSITION FINGERING

Ascending from open string: 0-1-1-2-2-3-4
Descending from fourth finger: 4-3-2-2-1-1-0

Also practice (1) slurring each two notes, and (2) slurring each four notes.

Extended Chromatic Scale